THE PINK ELEPHANT

A PRACTICAL GUIDE TO CREATING AN ANTI-RACIST ORGANIZATION

by
Janice Z. Gassam Asare, Ph.D.

Janice Z. Gassam Asare, Ph.D. © 2020

Book design: Shantia Coleman

Editor: Debra Palmer

ISBN: 978-0-578-79129-6

Because of the dynamic nature of the internet, any web addresses or links contained in this book may have changed since publication and may no longer be valid. The views expressed in this work are solely those of the author and do not necessarily reflect the views of the publisher, and the publisher disclaims any responsibility for them.

Printed in the United States of America.

www.drjanicegassam.com

DEDICATION

This book is dedicated to Breonna Taylor. Although I did not know you personally, I feel like I did. Your life mattered. Your story mattered. Your death shook the world and I will continue to fight for you. The work that I do is in your honor. The most basic human right is the right to life. Many of us have felt like we are fighting and shouting so that we are given this most basic human right. If we do not have the right to live, what do we have? Your story broke the world's heart. Your passion for helping others likely drove you to your career as an emergency medical technician. Thank you for saving lives even though yours was taken with such little regard. I hope we make you proud. We will keep your legacy alive and your name and story will be painted on our hearts and our minds forever. We will not forget you, Breonna. I will not forget you.

I write this with the understanding that one day I will no longer be here. I write these words to immortalize these thoughts. I hope that this book lands in the hands of someone who will use it to change the world.

TABLE OF CONTENTS

Introduction

Four months after the murder of George Floyd, I posted a poll on my LinkedIn account asking my followers about shifts that their company has made in what I've dubbed as the Racial Revolution of 2020. Of the 188 followers who answered, 7% said that their organization has made a lot of progress, 29% indicated some progress has been made, while the remaining 64% said their company has made little progress or no progress. This book was written to move organizations away from making empty statements with little action to rolling up their proverbial sleeves and doing the work that it will take to build an anti-racist organization.

I've been curating conversations about race, racism, and Black identity on my YouTube channel since 2011. I've been an educator for six years. My start in racial equity research began in 2014 when I was enrolled in a diversity, equity and inclusion (DEI) course for my doctoral program. I've always been what some might call "race obsessed" from an early age, having to navigate American culture while being Black in mostly white spaces while also trying to understand my parents' Cameroonian culture. In 2014 in my DEI course I decided to write my final paper on Black women and our unique experiences in the workplace. My professor gave me glowing remarks when I turned in my final paper and indicated that it was one of the strongest papers he had read thus far. I think it was at that point that you could say my journey in racial equity work was catalyzed. I thought the unique challenges that Black women faced like hair discrimination and the angry black woman trope were common knowledge to everyone but my professor's reaction let me know that more work was needed to educate the masses on racial equity.

Following the killing of George Floyd in May of 2020, the ghosts of America's past have come back to haunt the country, which never fully reconciled the greatest atrocity in American history. Since the Racial Revolution of 2020 began, I have conducted over 50 different workshops specifically on anti-racism and racial equity in the workplace. Requests for my racial equity workshops have increased exponentially, to the point where I cannot currently keep up with demand and have started to funnel requests to other Black, Indigenous and People of Color (BIPOC) practitioners and consultants in the field. I felt it was imperative to write this book because it's obvious that more work in corporate America is needed, around racial understanding and reconciliation. People are still confused about how to have effective and constructive conversations about race that build understanding, fosters inclusion and belonging. This book was written for anyone hoping to learn more about how to have discussions about race at work, in an environment that has not always been welcoming of these sorts of conversations. In the new world we are currently living in, where remote work has become the new norm, the need for effective racial dialogue and understanding how to address racial microaggressions online, is ever-present. By the end of this book, I want you to walk away with a) an understanding of the history of xenophobia in the U.S., b) a recognition of how structural and systemic racism manifests in the U.S. c) strategies for more effective racial dialogue and what behaviors and actions to avoid, d) how to support Black employees, and e) some common answers to frequently asked questions on race and diversity.

I have had the pleasure to collaborate with some well-known companies and institutions including Amazon, Google, Nordstrom, Papa John's, Yale University, the Dr. Oz Show and H&M. I've learned a lot along the way and feel that it's imperative to share what I've learned on this journey thus far. My hope is that this book will be a guide for you to build an anti-racist workplace. As a thank you for purchasing this book, I am also providing you with a free checklist as you start or continue your journey to becoming an anti-racist organization. The checklist can be found at www.drjanicegassam.com/antiracism.

CHAPTER 1

⤜⥈⥈⟡⥈⥈⤛

WHY IS RACE SO
HARD TO TALK ABOUT?

Race is like a hot pink elephant. Imagine how difficult it would be to ignore a hot pink elephant that walks into a room. You pretend it's not there and you don't see it, but you do from the corner of your eye. How silly is it to pretend you don't see the hot pink elephant? That's how many organizations operate. Race has become the hot pink elephant that leaders and employees alike pretend they don't see because they're "colorblind". At some point in recent decades, this disturbing colorblind mantra has become the norm. I'm here to tell you that the goal is not and has never been colorblindness. If you have eyes to see, race will be one of the first defining factors that you notice about a person. Saying you don't see race is simply a fallacy. The goal is to recognize our unique racial differences but not allow these differences to influence our decision-making.

When I started doing workshops and training within corporations, I was almost always steered away from focusing on racial equity, white supremacy, and white privilege. When conversing with clients about what my workshops focused on, there has been a strategic effort by company leaders to direct (or rather redirect) my focus to topics like emotional intelligence, diversity of thought and gender diversity. While these topics are extremely important and necessary to focus on to create a more equitable and inclusive workplace, they are not the reasons we are in the conundrum that is our current reality. We, as a country, have shied away from talking about race and racism. There is an oft-quoted saying that those who do not learn from history will be doomed to repeat it. It is imperative for us, as a country, to learn and understand our history to have a deeper recognition of how systemic and structural racism has manifested for hundreds of years.

At a Black History Month event I attended years ago, one of the speakers said something that I'll never forget. He explained that he thinks it's so challenging for people to have racial dialogue because of the lack of relatability that people have towards communities of color. He gave an example that everyone knows someone who is a woman, so having discussions on gender equity is not challenging for people. In addition, many of us have friends or family who are a part of the LGBTQIA+ community, so solidarity and understanding with this community are again, less challenging for us. But when it comes to race, many of us only hang out with members of our own racial group and we don't have people in our immediate circle who are of different races, which makes racial understanding more challenging.

Corporate leaders may shy away from these particular conversations because of fears of offending others. In speaking with a number of white leaders who share their difficulties in this domain, there are genuine fears of saying the wrong thing and offending members of marginalized groups. These are legitimate concerns. If you have grown up in a society like the United States where anti-blackness and white supremacy have been ingrained into everything we do, it will take many years to unlearn what we've been programmed to do. And that is okay.

But we have to be willing to engage in the conversation if we are ever going to produce real and long term change.

White privilege is a topic that is sometimes challenging for white people to understand. White privilege can be thought of as the invisible access and opportunity afforded to white people simply because of their skin color. Examples of white privilege come in many forms. One can look no further than the inequities in sentencing rates of white and non-white criminals, the housing discrimination that still takes place in different parts of the country where Black homebuyers experience greater challenges with purchasing homes and securing funding for homes, and even the discrepancies in venture capital funding that business owners of color receive compared to their white counterparts. One of the main reasons why racial dialogue is challenging is because of the lack of understanding in regards to white privilege. Also, the conversation rarely extends further than the discussion of white privilege. In order to understand how to create a racially equitable organization, the conversation must be amended to include discussions about how one's privilege can be used to impact change (which we will discuss in later chapters).

Acknowledging privilege is hard. And many assume that having privilege means you did not work hard to get to where you are. That is a fallacy. You can still be a hardworking and tenacious individual who has simultaneously benefited from a system that upholds and advantages white people. This is one of the main reasons why white people struggle with conversations about race. Also, accompanied by these conversations may be a sense of guilt. Guilt around what was done to BIPOC in America and the horrible atrocity that was American slavery. Although we are roughly six generations removed from slavery and no one currently alive was an enslaved person, the impacts of slavery are still being felt in America today. Opening up a conversation about race can often spark white guilt which can then lead to defensiveness, denial and disagreements. The goal of racial dialogue should never be to place blame on one group or victimize another. It is impossible to undo the past but the start of change begins with awareness, acceptance, acknowledgment and accountability.

Understand that conversations about race, especially at first, will be challenging. You will likely say the wrong thing. We have to unlearn and undo a lifetime's worth of misconceptions and stereotypes that have shaped our biases and racism. I don't want you to feel guilty about what happened in the past. But I implore you to engage in dialogue with people from different backgrounds to bridge the gaps of misunderstanding. The similar-to-me effect is the phenomenon where people gravitate toward others who are similar to them. Not surprisingly, this manifests in several ways including our likelihood and propensity to forge bonds with individuals who are the same race as us. What this often translates to is lower numbers of cross-racial friendships and more homogeneity in our circles. If the majority of your friends look, talk, and think like you, it will be harder to break out of these ingrained patterns of thinking.

There is also an expectation that conversations about race should and will be simple. But the reality is that racial dialogue is complex, confusing and can challenge everything you've ever known but these conversations are necessary as we strive for greater understanding. I recognize that even as a DEI practitioner who does work around racial equity and inclusion, I still have my own blindspots and I try to adopt the mindset that sometimes, even though some people label me as a subject matter expert I will get things wrong. It's important to mention that I don't even really believe that people can be "experts" or even "subject matter experts" in racial equity. Everyone is an expert in their own experiences. What I would love to see more of is BIPOC being asked to facilitate discussions on race. BIPOC and particularly Black people are rarely seen as experts of our own oppression. If you look at many of the popular books on racism and racial bias, many of them are written by non-BIPOC authors. Disrupting racism and bias requires radical empathy and the ability to put yourself in the shoes of others. Without hearing personal narratives and anecdotes of how people experience racism in various forms, it's harder to empathize and understand another person's experiences.

When you're in the midst of a conversation about race, remember a few things: it's going to be challenging, especially if this is the first conversation about race that you are having with someone. An important point to remember and note is that change does not occur through comfortability. A predecessor to growth and development is uncomfortability. Remove the expectation that the discussion will be easy; it won't be. There's also a possibility that it will not be a productive dialogue (we will explore strategies to utilize for more productive dialogue in later chapters). But what you're ultimately doing is planting seeds, which will hopefully grow and manifest into change. But no change can happen if you're too afraid, nervous or apprehensive to have the conversation.

The Racial Revolution of 2020 allowed the world, and particularly the U.S., to see that we can't keep running from conversations about race. You likely picked up this book because you wanted guidelines to navigate racial dialogue at work. Maybe you want to gain a better understanding of how to support your colleagues of color. Perhaps you're trying to foster an organizational culture that promotes racial equity. Whatever the reason you picked up this book, you must realize that the first part of creating an anti-racist organization is recognizing the history and how racial groups have been systematically and historically disadvantaged in the United States for centuries. We will briefly explore the history and examine how to recognize and be aware of our own biases. We will also explore strategies for effective racial dialogue and examine ways that we can use our power and privilege to create change.

CHAPTER 2

A VERY BRIEF HISTORY OF SYSTEMIC RACISM IN THE UNITED STATES

I n order to understand how to create a work-place that fosters racial equity and inclusion, it's imperative to understand how past practices, policies, and laws systematically disadvantaged different racial groups. This chapter examines a few major moments that contributed to the societal racism of different groups. To unlearn our own racial biases, we must first recognize the countless ways that systems have been structured to harm BIPOC. These moments are in chronological order and are by no means exhaustive or extensive. I chose to highlight these particular cases because of the trickle-down effects that they had on different racial groups. I will very briefly describe these moments and highlight their long term implications. I encourage you to learn and read more about each of these.

- **Indian Removal Act of 1830**: Based on this law, which was endorsed by President Andrew Jackson, Indigenous peoples of the United States were forcibly removed from their lands and had to walk across several states to their designated territory. Many suffered from hunger, disease, and even death on their voyage[1].

  Trickle-down effect: Indigenous peoples in the U.S. still currently experience several challenges including poverty, unemployment, and higher rates of adverse health conditions.

- **Special Order No. 15**: Based on this 1865 policy, enslaved African people were supposed to receive 40 acres of the southern land. When Andrew Johnson became president following Abraham Lincoln's assassination, this order was rescinded and therefore never came to fruition[2].

Trickle-down effect: Black people in the U.S. never received the "40 acres and a mule" that were promised to them. Black people were unable to accumulate wealth at comparable rates to their white counterparts which contributes to the racial wealth gap. One of the best ways to build wealth is via property. Black people being denied the rights to own property through discriminatory housing practices and being denied land that was rightfully owed to them for centuries of free labor has slowed Black economic progress and has created additional barriers to wealth building.

- **Chinese Exclusion Act**: Based on this 1882 law, Chinese people were not allowed to immigrate to the United States$_3$.

Trickle-down effect: Xenophobia and racism against Asian people still takes place and were evident in early 2020 when Covid-19 spread across the United States. East Asians have been labeled the model minority and there is a false perception in society that they do not experience discrimination but in the workplace, they must overcome the bamboo ceiling, which is the invisible barrier that they face in the workplace. East Asians experience challenges when trying to ascend into leadership positions largely because of the false perception that Asians do not possess leadership skills.

- **Separate but Equal**: Based on the Plessy versus Ferguson case in 1896 where The Supreme Court agreed that segregation was legal because although Black and white institutions and facilities were separate they were "equal$_4$."

Trickle-down effect: Although Plessy versus Ferguson was overturned by The Supreme Court, legal forms of it still take place today. Integration was mandated more than 50 years ago, but conditions in mostly BIPOC versus white neighborhoods are not the same. Forced integration gave a false belief that things were going to be equal but they are still inequitable today. Property values in white neighborhoods tend to be higher, on average, than majority-BIPOC neighborhoods. Property values determine how much funding public schools receive, causing obvious disparities in educational funding for certain school districts.

- **The Immigration Act of 1924**: Under this legislation, which was passed under President Calvin Coolidge, immigrants from certain parts of the world were prohibited from entering the United States. It's important to note that this act did not exclude all foreigners from entering the U.S. but was supposed to encourage merit-based immigration that prioritized the highly skilled and college-educated. It ended up being seen as a racially discriminatory and xenophobic policy[5].

Trickle-down effect: The Immigration Act of 1924 set a precedence for similar bans. In 2017, President Trump signed an executive order that placed a travel ban on people entering the U.S. from certain majority-Muslim countries. There have been several iterations of the travel ban since 2017 and it has been criticized as xenophobic and discriminatory.

There are so many events that have happened in U.S. history that have vastly shaped society now. When having a discussion about systemic racism and privilege and how to create policies and practices in the workplace that promote equity, there needs to be an understanding of how BIPOC have been negatively impacted by different policies. Before attempting to design and develop programs that promote equity and inclusion, I encourage you to learn more about the history of different racial groups in the U.S. The average child is not taught about the reverberating effects of racism in America. And that's a large part of the problem. Without having a thorough understanding of why and how the problem exists, it will be challenging to even recognize how to develop solutions to address these issues.

Beyond reading a book or watching a movie about something, encourage people in your workplace to have civil discourse around media and content that are being consumed. I encourage organizations to host an activity I created called **Consume,**

Digest & Dialogue (CDD). This is a facilitated discussion where employees are invited to consume a piece of historical content (movie, video, TV show, podcast, article, social media post, etc.), digest what they have seen or heard and then discuss their interpretations, understanding and what they have learned with fellow employees. There is so much content out there in the world and there are so many mediums for learning and consuming information. The purpose of the CDD is to spark meaningful conversations about history and relevant topics that may be more challenging and sensitive. Sometimes it's difficult to open up a conversation with a coworker about your views on racism but when you've watched a TV show that examines these topics in more depth, it allows individuals to have an opportunity to open up a discourse. During a CDD, some important questions to consider include:

1. What was the overall message you gained from this piece of content?
2. How does the issue of racism show up in this content?

3. What does this content teach me about what different racial groups have had to endure?

4. How does this content challenge my understanding and perspective?

An important distinction must be made when examining and assessing history. In the past, many of the great leaders of the Civil Rights movement spoke of equality and how that was one of the goals behind the movement. This narrative still echoes today: that BIPOC just want to be treated equally. But in our workplaces, we should be focusing on equity rather than equality. Equality is the act of treating everyone the same. Equity takes it a step further and considers the unique challenges that people of different groups have experienced. Learning the history of racism in the U.S. will help you understand some of the longstanding issues that marginalized groups have had to face. Knowledge of these unique challenges will help you understand how to create systems and structures that specifically address these challenges.

CHAPTER 3

DISRUPTING AND DISMAN-
TLING WHITE SUPREMACY

I t is impossible to discuss racial equity without uncovering, understanding, and unpacking the role that white supremacy has played in upholding systems of oppression. White supremacy can be thought of as the belief that white people are better than or superior to all other races. White supremacy permeates every system and structure within the United States and beyond. A belief in white supremacy along with practices and policies that reinforce white supremacy must be examined and unlearned for racial equity to be achieved. What is important to understand is that if the goal is to disrupt, deconstruct and dismantle racism, then white supremacy must be called out for what it is. In the past, there has been some hesitance to even use the term *white supremacy*, because of fears of public backlash. Racial equity requires nuanced conversations that neither sugarcoat nor soften the insidious nature of white supremacy. One of the ways that white supremacy is protected is in our language and how we describe and conceptualize white supremacy. White supremacy is not just white hoods and cross burning or those who oppose the removal of confederate monuments. The belief that white supremacy takes only this form is one of the reasons why it has been able to morph and shapeshift throughout the centuries. White supremacy continues to elude many of us because of the lack of understanding regarding how white supremacy is manifested.

In *Letter from Birmingham Jail,* Martin Luther King Jr. shared his thoughts on white moderates. King explained the danger of many white moderates, who insist on keeping the order rather than freeing marginalized people from oppression and went on to say that this is one of the greatest threats to racial progress. Those of the majority who choose to dictate how and when freedom should be fought for are the biggest threats we must watch out for. There is a commonly held belief that the election of Donald J. Trump in 2016 catalyzed white supremacy in the U.S. What's important to understand is that white supremacy existed before Trump and will continue after he has left office. We must disassociate the ideology from politics and people. Having good intentions or adopting a certain political ideology doesn't absolve you of racism or make you an anti-racist. We must first accept that those who grew up in American society have been indoctrinated into a pervasive belief system. Even people of color uphold systems of white supremacy and anti-black racism. This is explained in more detail in upcoming chapters. Creating an anti-racist organization requires the understanding that we have all contributed to white supremacy as a system. Understanding our blind spots is the first step to racial equity within the workplace.

When engaging in racial dialogue, we must be able to call out white supremacy for what it is. In 2020, the term *Karen* was popularized and refers to a middle-aged white woman who displays racist behavior that often involves calling the police on an innocent person of color. While some people have said that they consider the term to be a slur, the reality is that it is a euphemism compared to pejoratives that have been used against people of color.

We must not be afraid to call racism out for what it is. To paraphrase author Reni Eddo-Lodge, when we call out racism for what it is we are chipping away at its power. We must first have a full understanding of what racism even is. Racism can be thought of as the combination of systems of power and privilege that work in tandem to oppress BIPOC. Based on this definition, BIPOC cannot be racist in a society where they are not in a position of power. Anyone, no matter the race can, however, hold prejudiced and biased points of view but based on this definition, cannot be racist. We must understand that racism is not just ill will or bad feelings towards a non-white person but include the systems and structures that work to oppress these same people, which we will talk in more detail about in later chapters. It's impossible to grow up in a country that was built and founded on racism without internalizing the racism ourselves. My objective is not to make you feel bad for the racist and white supremacist ideologies that you may continuously uphold. My goal is to a) help you uncover and understand the many ways that white supremacy works to disadvantage BIPOC, b) examine your internalized racism and where it may come from and c) equip you with the tools to dismantle racism in your workplace.

Researcher Andrea Smith outlined three pillars of white supremacy[2]. The first pillar is based on the notion that Black people are property and are enslavable. Although American slavery has ended, Smith indicates that the prison industrial complex could be considered a new form of slavery. The second pillar of white supremacy is based on the idea that Indigenous populations must be eradicated and that their land should be taken. The theory of Manifest Destiny is a good example of this pillar in action. Manifest Destiny was a belief that it was the divine right of the U.S. to spread its reach and dominance across North America. The third pillar of white supremacy is based on the notion that people from Asia are inferior to their white counterparts. Many past laws and policies within the United States have exemplified the manifestation of each pillar. The third pillar was personified through the Chinese Exclusion Act and the internment of Japanese Americans during World War II.

White supremacy is predicated on the belief that all other races are inferior to whites and that white people should assert dominance over other races.

For white supremacy to continue, there must always be a perceived subordinate race or caste to subjugate. To dismantle white supremacy, it will not only take BIPOC, but white people also speaking up and speaking out against white supremacy while simultaneously working to transform the systems and structures that allow white supremacy to continue. Eradicating systemic racism is in white people's best interest. Here are some reasons why white people will actually benefit from dismantling white supremacy and working towards anti-racism.

1. Demographers predict that around the year 2045 the United States will be majority non-white. As the population becomes more racially diverse due to the rapid growth of the population of mixed-race people, it becomes even more vital for everyone to learn how to live in the country cohesively. When we are divided as a nation, we cannot thrive.

2. A 2019 racial wealth gap study by McKinsey & Company[3] found that closing the racial wealth gap would not only positively impact Black communities but would also add an estimated $1-1.5 trillion to the U.S. economy by the year 2028. Closing the racial

wealth gap would positively impact everyone living in the U.S.

3. Planet Earth is also suffering from the continuation of systemic racism. Environmental racism allows white supremacy to continue. Environmental racism is a form of systemic racism in which predominantly BIPOC communities are more likely to be hazard zones. Areas where BIPOC live tend to be deemed as wastelands where little regard is given to the impacts of different environmental decisions. The Flint, Michigan water crisis is an appropriate example of how environmental racism disproportionately impacts communities of color. The water in Flint, Michigan was contaminated with lead, imperiling the health of city residents. A majority of the residents in Flint, at the time of the water crisis, were Black. The disregard of certain areas that are highly populated by BIPOC not only impacts the people living in those communities but has a detrimental effect on the planet as a whole, which ultimately affects everyone.

4. White supremacy is predicated on the belief that white people must fit a prototype to reap the benefits of white privilege. Any person, who doesn't fit this prototype will be marginalized and oppressed. The white prototype is what is seen as the norm and the default. We apply white norms to everything and it is often used as a metric for success, across races. As a BIPOC, if you move to a neighborhood with a high population of white people, you are seen as successful. Also, if you receive an award or acknowledgment by a well-known white institution or foundation, it is a mark of success and status. Anything outside of white norms is not uplifted or awarded in our society. White supremacy should be in every person's interest to dismantle because any white person can find themselves in a position where they no longer fit this prototype. In order for white supremacy to continue and thrive, there must be marginalized groups to oppress and apply these white norms to. Any person who belongs to an oppressed community is negatively impact-

ed by white supremacy, which is predicated on the belief that white people are genetically and intellectually superior to all other races of people. Based on these tenets, any person who finds themselves outside of these white norms may experience othering and discrimination. Ableism is the discrimination faced by people with disabilities. Any white person can experience ableism and may be stigmatized based on their disability status. This is not to say a disabled person cannot be a white supremacist but having an understanding of how oppression continues should allow everyone to understand why white supremacy will not and does not benefit anyone. Additionally, as we get older, age discrimination becomes a very real issue that anyone can face. The idea of white people being the master race perpetuates the belief that to fit this prototype, a white person must be strong, intelligent and able-bodied. Those that do not fit this prototype are negatively impacted by the continuation of white supremacy. Deconstructing oppressive systems will benefit white people because white supremacy forces everyone to chase unrealistic and unattainable white norms and standards or face harsh consequences for not adhering to and modeling these standards. Anyone can find themselves deviating from what is deemed as the pinnacle of white perfection. Freedom and liberation of all marginalized groups are predicated on shattering and dismantling white supremacy.

White supremacy is habitual. White is the norm and anything outside of that, we denigrate. As long as we have eyes to see, we will always be able to recognize different skin shades and tones. The ultimate goal is to not allow this recognition to taint our perception of others and thus control our actions and behaviors towards members of these groups. Understanding white supremacy requires a deep understanding of how we uphold oppressive systems but also how we are all disadvantaged by the continuation of these systems. We must first recognize the ways that these systems work to keep people oppressed in the subordinate caste, a term I became familiar with in Isabel Wilkerson's book, *Caste*. In the book, Wilkerson explains how the United States has a caste system that is comparable to other societies. Based on this American caste system, which can be conceptualized as a system of oppression, Black Americans are part of the subordinate caste and are the most oppressed and marginalized group. Dismantling the whole system requires an understanding of how these systems work to continue to marginalize different groups.

CHAPTER 4

——◆◆◆——

UNDERSTANDING AND UN-PACKING YOUR PRIVILEGE

Dismantling, disrupting, and deconstructing white supremacy and creating a more equitable organization requires a thorough understanding of our individual blind spots and privileges. I know that when you hear the word privilege, you automatically think about white privilege. That is a very real thing, whether you know it or not. White privilege can manifest in a number of different ways. In the U.S. criminal justice system, evidence of white privilege is everywhere. A few important cases to explore: juxtapose the cases of Felicity Huffman and Lori Loughlin, two white actresses embroiled in the college admissions scandal (2019)[1] with the case of a Black mother Kelley Williams-Bolar (2011)[2] who received jail time for falsifying her child's address to get into a better school district. In addition, examine the cases of Justine Ruszczyk, an unarmed white woman from Australia who was fatally shot by Mohamed Noor, a Black Muslim police officer in Minneapolis (2017)[3]. Noor was convicted of third-degree murder, which carries a sentence of between 10-25 years in prison. Compare this with the tragic shooting of Amadou Diallo (1999), a 23-year old who immigrated to New York from the West African country of Guinea. Diallo was shot by four white officers that confused Diallo for a rape suspect. All four officers were acquitted of all charges[4]. Breonna Taylor (2020) was a 26-year-old emergency medical technician who was fatally shot in her own home while sleeping when police came to serve a search warrant for her apartment. Taylor's boyfriend, who had a legally obtained firearm, fired a warning shot when police arrived and did not announce themselves[5]. Police claim they *did* announce their arrival but witnesses say they did not. A grand jury decided not to pursue any homicide charges for the three officers involved in Taylor's case, who all happen to be white. The system rarely seems to work for BI-POC.

To further understand how white privilege has given disproportionate advantages to white people who have committed heinous crimes, it is important to examine the tragic 2015 shooting at Emanuel African Methodist Episcopal Church in Charleston, South Carolina by Dylann Roof. Roof was a then-21-year-old who killed nine Black people during Bible study[6]. When Roof was arrested, reports indicated that officers bought him food from Burger King following his arrest[7]. This angered many because of the inhumane treatment that is often experienced by Black suspects after they are arrested. Compare the arrest of Roof to that of George Floyd in 2020, whose only crime was allegedly using a counterfeit $20 bill to pay for a convenience store purchase[8]. Floyd was apprehended by officer Derek Chauvin in the now infamous video where he kneeled on Floyd's neck for almost nine minutes, killing him. It leaves us to wonder whether Floyd would still be alive right now, had his skin been a different color. The differential treatment of the suspects in these cases provides evidence for how white privilege can prove deadly.

These cases of white privilege and differential treatment are just the tip of the iceberg. If this book was dedicated to examples of white privilege, it would be hundreds of thousands of pages long. Anyone who denies that being white affords a person unearned access and opportunity is choosing a path of willful ignorance. Privilege, contrary to popular myths, has nothing to do with a person's financial status or standing. As a blue-collar worker, your skin still grants you access, opportunity, advantages, and privileges that others do not have. In 2009, Harvard University professor Henry Louis Gates Jr. was arrested after a Cambridge Police Department officer thought Gates had broken into his own home after Gates' door was jammed$_9$. Gates is a well-known historian, author, and teacher, who hosts the show *Finding Your Roots* on PBS. Gates showed the officer his Massachusetts driver's license and Harvard University ID card but that did not suffice for the officer, who claims that a white woman had called the police after seeing two suspicious Black men attempting to enter the home. If a person of Gates' status was still subjected to inequitable treatment, that should be a clear indication that white privilege spans beyond wealth and notoriety. As a white person, hoping to create an antiracist organization, there must be an acknowledgment and understanding of how your skin grants you advantages that BIPOC do not have.

An important part of the privilege discussion expands beyond white privilege. The unspoken advantage that is granted to white people in society must be unpacked. But each of us, in different ways, also has privilege, access and opportunities that are important to examine. As a Black woman who strives to help others unpack and unlearn their biases, I had to engage in an unpacking and unlearning process myself. As a light-skinned Black woman who grew up in majority-white spaces, I never knew about colorism and how rampant it is until I was in mostly-Black spaces. Dismantling racism also involves deconstructing how we perpetuate anti-blackness within communities of color. Privilege isn't just white privilege. As a lighter skinned Black woman, I have privilege based on my proximity to whiteness. It's important to explore some terminology to better understand privilege beyond just the scope of white privilege: White adjacency is necessary to discuss. I want you to conceptualize white adjacency as the invisible access that a person of color has based on their proximity to and alignment with whiteness. It is difficult to ascertain the origin of the term, but according to the Urban Dictionary website, a user named MARI99 in 2017 defined white adjacency as distancing yourself from your race and engaging in activities that allow you to assimilate into white society$_{10}$. I understand that white adjacency may be considered by some to be a survival technique. In a world that prioritizes whiteness, attaching oneself to whiteness seemingly produces many benefits. An example of white adjacency is a White Hispanic woman with more Eurocentric features such as light eyes, light hair, and a European phenotype who does not correct coworkers who mistake her for a white person. White adjacency is another manifestation of white supremacy. Based on the perception that aligning with one's own race will not produce the desired results, a person distances themselves from their race. As a person of color reading this, please understand that you can still perpetuate anti-black racism as a non-black person of color. Based on the updated definition of racism, systems of power and privilege work in tandem to oppress those in the subordinate racial caste. Under this definition, Black Indigenous People of Color cannot be racist but I *do* want to point out that BIPOC can still be anti-black. Dismantling racism must also mean disrupting and deconstructing our anti-black racism.

Anti-blackness is rampant within communities of color. George Lopez provided us with an example of this in 2017 when he made a joke about how Mexican parents don't want you to bring a Black person home. It is often said that there is truth in jest. Lopez's joke reflects the beliefs and feelings of many communities of color. Colorism and anti-blackness have manifested in several ways from India's caste system to the popularity of skin-bleaching creams in Latin America and Africa. Unpacking our privilege involves recognizing and understanding ways that we have perpetuated anti-black racism, which may have been learned from the media, our friends or our families. Unpacking your privilege involves exploring the question- who does not have the same privileges that I have right now? In asking myself this question, I was able to write down several privileges that I have and that I can use to advocate for others who don't have the same privileges. Some privileges that I currently have include:

- Light-skinned privilege
- Straight/cisgender privilege

- Weight privilege
- Able-bodied privilege
- Education privilege

I also recognize that coming from a two-parent household, where I lived in middle-class neighborhoods for the majority of my childhood afforded me many privileges that I cannot take for granted. I encourage you to do two things: 1) Write down all of the ways that you have access, opportunities and privileges that others may not have and 2) think about how you can use these privileges to impact change and advocate for others.

Example:

Privilege
- Light-skinned privilege

How I try to use this privilege to impact change
- Have open discussions about colorism in my anti-racism workshops/trainings
- Writing about colorism in my articles
- Using my voice and access to advocate for and amplify

- Calling out colorism when I see it (in-person and via social media)
- Using images that contain more skin tone diversity in my classroom lectures, workshops, and articles.

As an anti-racism educator and diversity, equity and inclusion consultant, I feel it's important for me to constantly be aware of and recognize blind spots that I may have. I recently took Harvard University's Implicit Association Test (IAT), which I recommend everyone to take. I took the test on skin tone bias and learned that I have a strong automatic preference toward lighter skin tones. I was expecting my results to indicate that I had little to no preference toward dark or light skin tones. Awareness of our blind spots is the first step to create an anti-racist workplace. It's likely that we're engaging in biased behaviors based on our lack of awareness of our blind spots and the stereotypes we have about other groups. Racial equity is not a finite point but rather a lifelong journey for organizations. I like to consider anti-racism a muscle that must continuously be strengthened to grow and remain strong. To strengthen your anti-racism muscles, you must first uncover and unpack your privilege. The next step is recognizing how to use your privilege to advocate for others. Some suggestions I can offer include:

- Making introductions via email or LinkedIn to expand a person's network and impact their job prospects. 80-85% of all jobs are now found through referrals. Use your privilege by expanding another person's network and making virtual introductions to changemakers within your network that others would benefit from being acquainted with.

- Amplify the work of BIPOC. Share articles, podcasts, online courses, books, and other creative works that were designed by BIPOC. You may be instrumental in introducing your network to a BIPOC creative that was not on a person's radar

- Donate your time, money and resources to supporting BIPOC businesses. It should come as no surprise that many business owners of color experience barriers when it comes to securing venture capital funding. Patronize businesses owned by BIPOC and share these businesses with friends and family

- Use your privilege to speak out and speak up when you witness racism taking place. That may be speaking up for someone in the boardroom or it could be defending someone who is a victim of racial microaggressions. It could also be calling out racism on social media or in virtual settings. There are several ways to use your voice to amplify the voices of marginalized people.

CHAPTER 5

---⬥◈◈◈⬥---

STRATEGIES FOR
EFFECTIVE RACIAL DIALOGUE

One of the questions I get asked the most frequently is how to have effective discussions about race. When engaging in racial dialogue with a BIPOC, it's helpful to remember **A.D.R.** which stands for assess, discuss and repeat.

Assess: Evaluate whether you and the other person/people are in the right state to have an open conversation about race. In moments when I find myself feeling tired or highly stressed, I often refrain from having these heavier conversations. As a BIPOC, you have to ask yourself whether you are ready to engage in these types of conversations, which can be laborious and energy-consuming. It's always a good idea to be mindful of your own mindstate but also to be aware of the mindstate that the other person is in.

Discuss: If you decide to engage in the conversation, share your feelings and thoughts with your counterparts and also be sure to allow the same consideration through active listening. The most vital aspect of racial dialogue is listening. Without feeling the need to defend yourself, center your feelings, or dismiss the other person's feelings, unpack what was said during the conversation. In your head, ask yourself if you understand what was said, why the other person feels the way they feel and what part you may have played. Avoiding these discussions will obviously not lead to any sort of resolution.

Repeat: I think when having conversations about race and racism, repetition can be helpful. I like to repeat critical parts of what a person has shared with me to ensure I understand what was shared. When I'm engaged in a discussion with someone, when there is an acknowledgment of what I have shared and some sort of repetition, it makes me feel heard. It's vital to take in what you are being told and what is being shared in a conversation and utilizing repetition serves as a good way to clarify your understanding.

At work, use the ADR method to help guide your conversations. Some additional considerations to be mindful of when engaged in racial dialogue:

1. Don't force a BIPOC to engage in racial dialogue if they do not want to. This is an important rule of thumb you should highlight. If you are ever in a situation where you witness racial discrimination taking place, it is imperative to speak out and speak up, however, you should not force a BIPOC to engage in racial dialogue if they do not want to. BIPOC employees may face harsh consequences for speaking out and speaking up against racism. There could be a myriad of reasons why a BIPOC is not speaking up about the racism they have experienced. Be mindful of this and don't force a BIPOC to speak on a situation or about a situation before the person is ready. If you are a white person, you must use your voice, your power and your privilege to amplify BIPOC if

you ever witness, overhear or see racism taking place.

2. Listen without interrupting and wait 10 seconds before responding. In my first book *Dirty Diversity*, I shared the importance of waiting at least five seconds before responding when engaged in a conversation with someone you don't see eye to eye with. When it comes to discussions about race, I would encourage you to utilize the 10-second method where you wait 10 seconds before responding. A large part of the reason why conversations about race go awry is that when a BIPOC is sharing their experience with racial discrimination or microaggressions, the aggressor doesn't take in what is being said and may be too busy formulating a response, an excuse or a reason for what was said or done. When you don't listen to a person sharing their personal experiences with racism, you are missing out on an opportunity for development and growth. To be frank, anti-racism will not come from ignoring or invalidating victims of racism. When someone has trusted

you enough to share an experience of racial discrimination with you, this is a learning and growth opportunity. Adopting the 10-second strategy will mitigate your desire to engage in derailing behaviors that sidetrack a conversation.

3. When you are confronted with something you've done or said that a person deemed as racist, listen to what is being shared with you and then repeat what is being said to ensure you understand why it was offensive and problematic. For example, if your coworker Linda shares that your comment about her being articulate was a microaggression (because it implied that she was a deviation from the norm and that other people from her racial background were not articulate) listen to what is being said and repeat what has been explained and also think about how you will commit to doing better. It doesn't matter if it wasn't your intent to offend because as we all know, intent doesn't determine impact.

4. Don't expect a BIPOC to teach you everything there is to know about race. Aside

from not forcing BIPOC into conversations about race against their will, don't expect a BIPOC to teach you all there is to learn and understand about race. If you're confused about something, an online search will likely reveal a think-piece written about your exact inquiry. Actively seek out information that will help you expand your knowledge and awareness of people from races outside of your own.

5. If someone is offended by something, it was offensive. Point blank period. It doesn't matter if you don't understand how or why what was said was offensive. If anyone took offense to it, that should be taken into consideration. What you feel and think doesn't matter in that moment if you've said or done something to offend someone.

6. You're going to make mistakes. One book, one article or one documentary is not going to immediately shift your behavior, your perspective and your understanding. I still make mistakes, even as an anti-racism educator and DEI consultant. You must be open to correcting your mistakes and realiz-

ing that the goal is not to be correct or right but rather to reach a point of greater understanding and awareness and that is accompanied by correction.

7. Don't stop having the conversation. What happens sometimes is that the first time a conversation about race occurs, it may lead to arguments, disputes and disagreements. It happens when people don't see eye to eye. But that doesn't mean you should give up and not continue the conversation. I think everyone has the capacity to change; some people take longer than others, and some people may not actually change. I always keep in mind that the goal of racial dialogue is ultimately to plant seeds that will hopefully manifest and grow into greater understanding and awareness. Ideally, having a conversation will help a person come to a deeper understanding of how a mindset or a certain way of thinking requires a shift. Change takes time so it's important not to be deterred in your journey to greater understanding.

8. Lastly, it's important to be very specific when it comes to who and what you are talking about. Rather than using the umbrella term of BIPOC, being very specific in conversations about race is beneficial. If something that was said or done is offensive to a particular community, it's important to understand the specific significance of what was said and how it impacts that particular community. Also important to note is that it's not a BIPOC's job to educate and teach other people about their culture. Some BIPOC are open to educating you on cultural nuances, but that should not be the expectation. Also, it is important to remember that just because your friend of a particular racial background is okay with something and doesn't consider it to be offensive does not mean that it is not offensive. It should go without saying that the "but I have Black friends" excuse holds little value and weight. If you've done something that is offensive to Black people, it doesn't matter that your one Black friend is okay with your actions.

What to do when your racism is called out

When someone points out that you've behaved in discriminatory ways, it's important to remember the acronym **A.O.C.** This stands for accept, own, and correct. **Accept** what is being said and how, even though it may not have been your intent, that you still caused undue harm to another person or group of people through your behaviors and actions. **Own** what is being said. Take ownership and accountability for your actions. Lastly, think about how to **correct** the action to prevent it from happening in the future. Remember: You may not always be given information about how to correct your behavior when someone calls you out for racism or discrimination. If BIPOC had to explain to every single person who wronged them on how to correct their racist actions and behaviors, there wouldn't be time to do anything else. I encourage you not to ask BIPOC for free labor. Take on the responsibility of educating yourself to broaden your understanding.

Ideally, it's best to have racial dialogue in person. In a post-Covid-19 world, most people will continue working remotely at some level, so opportunities for in-person dialogue are becoming fewer and fewer. If the possibility of an in-person dialogue is not feasible, a virtual conversation is best. It's better when you can pick up on a person's facial expressions and body language. There are a plethora of options for a virtual conversation from WhatsApp video to Facetime to Zoom, Skype or WebEx.

We live in a social media world where much of the racism and racial dialogue that we witness taking place is online. The internet is the wild wild west. Before engaging in racial dialogue online, it's important to recognize a few things: a) some people are trolling to get a reaction out of others, b) the anonymity of the internet makes people feel more emboldened to say and do things they would never do in person. I don't want to say save your breath because there is value to online discourse but as you have probably realized already, civil discourse on social media is becoming rarer. As a general rule and policy of mine, I don't usually go back and forth with people especially when they say and do things that are clearly racist. The block and report buttons have become my best friends. I think it's important not to feed the trolls. By feed, I mean give them a reaction. I know sometimes it's hard to distinguish between who is interested in an honest exchange and conversation, versus who wants to get a rise out of you. I will engage with people online but if/when the conversation takes a turn where a person is name-calling, using illogical arguments to prove their point or trying to derail the discussion, I stop engaging. You have to use your discernment when it comes to figuring out who is worth engaging with and who is being a contrarian simply for attention, views, clicks and likes. I've noticed that attention has become one of the most coveted commodities. As a BIPOC, it's not your job or your duty to educate and engage with everyone. You have to do what's best for your mental wellbeing and for your energy. Sometimes for me, that's not even responding to the foolishness that I see directed at me. Other times, it's writing a term paper in my comment section to try to educate a person who is misinformed. Sometimes, it's an enlightening exchange where someone schools me and helps me to see things in a way I did not see before. When having racial dialogue online, tread cautiously.

As we move into a more virtual world, it is becoming increasingly more difficult to engage in civil discourse online. While I do believe that social media is a great place for learning and education to take place, the amount of noise from trolls on social media makes civil discourse more challenging. Race and politics are some of the most contentious topics to discuss online. I try to refrain from discussing politics online but race and politics are inextricably linked so it's challenging to talk about one without discussing the other. The more outspoken one is about social issues, the higher the likelihood of online harassment, bullying and other toxic behaviors. I recognize that simply through the publishing of this book, I am inviting conflict, criticism, and contention. But I do believe and hope that this book will be a catalyst for change that will positively impact this world. Trolls will always exist and the only way to avoid feeling their wrath is by doing nothing and saying nothing. Nearly a decade of being on YouTube has given me thick skin. I realize that there are some ways to engage in productive conversations online. If you find yourself in the middle of a racial discussion online here are a few tips I would recommend to ensure that the conversation is productive and keeps your energy intact with the rise of online trolling.

- Come with facts and figures. It's hard to argue with cold, hard evidence so when I post something, for example, and someone attempts to question the validity of the statements or the premise of my argument, I always try to provide information from reputable sources. Now, I understand that what we even deem as reputable varies and that's something important to consider and to remember. Be sure you are providing secondary and primary sources during these types of online discussions.

- I also love to cite videos in which someone has explained a concept or theory that is being discussed. There are countless videos on YouTube about a plethora of topics you may not have even considered. I would look at whether deep-dives are examining the topic(s) you are discussing online to provide others with greater insights.

- I like sharing experiences online and think there is some value to this. Anecdotes and first-hand accounts allow for greater empathy and understanding so whenever possible, I think sharing personal stories and experiences is good to include in an online dialogue about race.

- This should go without saying but sadly it does have to be said. Racial dialogue should be devoid of personal attacks and insults. Also, bringing irrelevant details into a conversation will inhibit productive dialogue, so it's important to avoid engaging in these activities, especially online.

- Lastly and probably the most important point to remember is some people are just trolling to get a reaction out of you and sway the conversation. I've often found that when someone seems to be arguing just for the sake of arguing without providing any evidence to corroborate their thoughts, feelings and opinions, they could be a bot or a troll, whose sole purpose is to derail, detract and distract from the conversation. When you find that someone is attempting to siphon your energy (I like to call them energy vampires) or engage you in a dialogue for their selfish purposes, also known as "clout chasing", I would stop the conversation. I like to exercise the block button and I block and report trolls who want to argue with me without presenting any information or further details to support their opinion. If you feel like the conversation is unproductive and energy-draining you can always refrain from engaging, which is a strategy I often practice.

There's a possibility that when employing these tactics, the other person or other people will be defensive, hateful and venomous. That's the point where I would disengage with them. I'm a firm believer in the idea that nothing put out into the world with pure intentions and love is ever wasted energy. When you do things from a pure place, it is time well spent. The time and energy I spend attempting to help shift a person's perspective is not a waste of time, even if in that moment it seems like the person is unreceptive and unmoved by the conversation. You are sowing seeds of change that may not see rapid growth at first but could eventually sprout into a shift.

CHAPTER 6

———◆◇◆———

RACIAL DIALOGUE
DETRACTIONS AND
DEFLECTIONS TO AVOID

The reason why you decided to read this book is likely because of this chapter right here. The number one question I hear asked both in my workshops and by friends and colleagues is "how do I have productive conversations about race?" Chapter 5 focused on strategies for productive racial dialogue. This chapter will focus on behaviors to avoid that can derail a conversation about race. I'm going to provide some examples of problematic behaviors that often occur when having a racial dialogue. These are terms I've used and the definitions given are my own interpretations of what each of these terms/phrases mean, based on my experiences. These definitions may slightly deviate from what you find through an online search.

White centering: This is the act of a white person refocusing a conversation on themselves when a BIPOC is sharing an experience. This often includes diverting a racial dialogue to discuss *your* feelings and emotions as a white person versus focusing on the feelings of BIPOC and what is being said.

Whataboutism: This is a deflection technique often used in racial dialogue to redirect the conversation to another group or issue, shifting the blame away from the initial person or people that the conversation was focused on. An example of this is when discussing police brutality against Black people, someone saying "well, what about Black on Black crime?" The reason why this particular whataboutism is problematic is that it does not consider the full story and the antecedents that lead to Black on Black crime. It is important to understand that crime is based on proximity and an overwhelming number of crimes against whites are committed by other whites. Due to systemic racism, Black people are more likely to live in poverty-stricken communities, which are more likely to experience crime. Poverty-stricken people are more likely to commit crimes compared to their counterparts. All of these factors are disregarded when this particular whataboutism about Black on Black crime is brought up.

White denial: I would describe this as a white person refusing to believe the experiences that a BIPOC is sharing in regards to racism. This may include statements like "I've been to that restaurant before...I don't think they're racist," to more extreme statements such as "systemic racism does not exist."

White gaze: This is the idea that white culture is the central culture from which everything must be viewed and understood. I conceptualize the white gaze as being a form of cultural hegemony, which is the idea that the dominant class frames the cultural views and understanding of all the other classes in a society. The idea behind cultural hegemony is that our perceptions are shaped by the dominant culture without us even realizing it. What is deemed as acceptable and expected in our culture, is seen through the white lens.

Tone policing: This involves the assumption that if a message is accompanied by emotion and is not delivered in a way that one deems appropriate, then the message loses its value. Telling a person to rephrase what they've said or saying something in "a nicer way" are some common examples of tone policing. Black Indigenous Women of Color (BIWOC) often experience tone policing.

Racial gaslighting: The act of denying that a person's racial experiences exist and making a person or group of people feel like they are overanalyzing a situation or that their experiences are not valid. This could involve statements like "Are you *sure* it was because of your race?" Essentially, I want you to conceptualize this as an invalidation of a person's experiences with racism.

White defensiveness: During conversations about what some would deem more sensitive and uncomfortable topics, defensiveness is a common side effect. This involves overreacting when a person shares an experience with racism. It often manifests as a person being quick to defend the racist person/behavior and may also involve providing excuses for why a person did or said what is being deemed as racist. When you haven't fully listened to or heard a person's experiences but you are quick to provide excuses as to why the experience was not racism, you are engaging in white defensiveness.

Adopting a fixed mindset: Having a fixed mindset will prohibit the necessary learning and growth that can be triggered by racial dialogue. I'm sure we've all heard someone excuse racist behavior by reasoning that because of their age, upbringing or where they grew up, they are incapable of changing their mindset. Although a person may have grown up during an era where certain things were more socially acceptable, racial awareness and understanding can be achieved at any age. Shift a fixed mindset to a growth mindset so you can be more open to the ability to change your current way of thinking.

Whitesplaining: This is another tactic used to divert a conversation that occurs when a white person attempts to explain racism to a BIPOC, often brushing off their experiences which can then turn into racial gaslighting. Whitesplaining may begin with a white person explaining why what they said or did was not racist followed by examples of their own interpretations of racism.

White saviorism: Often perpetuated in the media, white saviorism is the narrative/belief that white people must save, culture and civilize BIPOC. White saviorism is depicted in the media, especially in films. The white savior narrative in film typically involves a white person entering an environment or system and then saving the characters in the story. These types of movies often leave viewers feeling good and hopeful. What is problematic about these narratives is that they reinforce the belief that BIPOC are foreign, other and must be cultured and civilized. It does nothing to shatter the negative stereotypes about different cultures.

The weaponization of whiteness: Throughout history, we've seen countless examples of this. In recent years, we've seen an explosion of viral videos depicting white people calling the police on Black people for simply existing. While the viral videos are cringeworthy, they pale in comparison to what many Black people experienced before the age of social media and cell phones. A recognition of white privilege and utilizing it to wrongfully harm, vilify and incriminate BIPOC is how whiteness is weaponized. One of the most horrific examples of this was Emmett Till, who was a 14-year old boy wrongfully accused of whistling at a white woman. Till was viciously murdered. His accuser, on her deathbed, ended up admitting that she had lied about him whistling at her. The weaponization of whiteness is potentially deadly for BIPOC.

Racial minimization: A term I've coined to mean the act of downplaying racist historical events, particularly those that impact a subordinate racial group in society. Racial minimization can occur when a person engages in a discussion about a historical event like the Trail of Tears or American slavery. An example of racial minimization would be a person saying "why are you still talking about slavery? I didn't own slaves and you were not a slave!" A person who makes this statement is minimizing an event that had a drastic, long-lasting effect on Black people, while actively trying to belittle and demean a Black person's experience.

I want you to understand and memorize what each term means. Consider times when you may have engaged in these behaviors and how it can derail a conversation. If you're ever called out for any of these behaviors, please listen. Don't argue, don't get defensive, don't make excuses and don't minimize another person's feelings. Soak in what you are being told without feeling the need to respond or defend yourself. Bookmark this page and refer back to this list frequently.

CHAPTER 7

ANTI-RACISM EDUCATION
IN THE WORKPLACE

Creating an anti-racist organization requires a multi-pronged approach for employees and leadership. There are a number of different strategies that can be utilized for anti-racism education. The first option, and one of the more popular options for anti-racism education is via anti-racism workshops and training. Working as an anti-racism educator, there are several tools I have learned within the last few years that are helpful for organizations looking to implement anti-racism education into the diversity, equity and inclusion (DEI) toolbox. There are mixed reviews when it comes to DEI training. There are many studies that report that training is effective, while other research has indicated that these types of training sessions may cause hostility among different groups of employees. Anti-racism training exploded in popularity following the killing of George Floyd in May of 2020. The term anti-racism re-emerged in recent years because of author Ibram Kendi, who wrote the *New York Times* bestseller *How to be an Anti-racist.* Angela Y. Davis indicated that we cannot simply strive to not be racist but we must actively work to be anti-racists. Anti-racism can be thought of as actions and behaviors that actively work to dismantle racist systems of oppression. Because of the recent popularity of anti-racist training, I think it is imperative to share what has worked thus far for me during my anti-racism workshops. Leadership looking to implement anti-racism workshops and training sessions into the workplace can use this information when vetting anti-racism educators and trainers to assist the organization.

You first must consider whether it's best to utilize an external consultant or have your internal DEI head lead the anti-racism training. I have strong feelings about this. I truly believe that anti-racism training must be led by BIPOC practitioners. For far too long, white people have been seen as the sole experts in DEI and critical race theory. While I would never discount or discredit the studies conducted by white researchers and used several of these studies to write this book, one's personal experiences with racism can color the training in a more impactful way. As previously stated, BIPOC are rarely seen as experts of our own oppression so it's important to ensure that BIPOC experts are being utilized to conduct these training sessions. In addition, when going the route of anti-racism training and education, I think hiring an external consultant who has a particular expertise in that domain is the best strategy. DEI strategy entails company-wide policies that promote equity and inclusion but anti-racism focuses specifically on racial equity. Not all DEI practitioners are equipped to provide anti-racism training and education, which is why it's better to lean on the expertise of an anti-racism educator.

An anti-racism educator can provide employees with the historical background to understand how white supremacy has guided institutional policies in nearly every domain. It's challenging to be able to build on anti-racist practices without having a thorough understanding of the history. Learning the history and also engaging in perspective-taking activities where employees are able to listen to the stories and experiences of BIPOC can catalyze empathy, which leads to greater understanding and awareness. There are a number of different ways that history can be learned: books, television, films, podcasts, courses and first or secondhand accounts. Using a multi-pronged approach to learning that encompasses several methods is most effective.

It's important for anti-racism education to include a discussion about privilege. In my virtual anti-racism workshops, I created an activity called the **Advantage Awareness Activity (AAA)**. This is a modified version of the in-person exercise that is done to help participants conceptualize privilege by walking forward or back when a statement applies to them. The Advantage Awareness Activity is advantageous for online and virtual workshops. For the activity, I share a series of statements with participants. I ask that participants turn their camera on for the activity and that they raise their hands up to showcase their fingers. If a statement I read applies to them, I ask them to put a finger down. When everyone has their cameras on, as each person puts their finger down, this can be a powerful way for participants to conceptualize privilege. The statements should relate to different facets of a person's life including their educational experience, work experience, and upbringing, from a racial lens. Below is the Advantage Awareness Activity that I designed. This activity can be modified to fit any workplace or institution.

Suggested script: Instruct participants to turn their cameras on and raise their hands up so that they're in view of the camera. As you read the series of statements, ask participants to put a finger down if any of the following statements apply to them.

Statement 1: Put a finger down if you've ever been made fun of because of your race.

Statement 2: Put a finger down if you've ever felt passed over for a job because of the color of your skin.

Statement 3: Put a finger down if you've ever been followed before in a store.

Statement 4: Put a finger down if you've never had a grade school teacher that was the same race as you.

Statement 5: Put a finger down if your doctor is a different race than you.

Statement 6: Put a finger down if you spent the majority of your time in history classes learning about people of other races.

Statement 7: Put a finger down if you have ever been asked to speak on behalf of your racial group.

Statement 8: Put a finger down if you have ever been stopped by the police for no valid reason.

I encourage you to make this activity your own and add, modify or remove statements as you see fit. These are just some sample statements but you can add to these statements or modify them as you see fit.

An additional activity I suggest for everyone is the Harvard Implicit Association Test (IAT). This test can be found through an online search. It's a free test available online that helps you understand and become more aware of your implicit biases. I ask workshop attendees to take the IAT prior to the workshop and share their results, if they feel comfortable. The IAT is a great way to uncover our unconscious bias and we are immediately able to assess whether we have an automatic preference for different groups of people. The AAA coupled with the IAT can provide deeper insight into our conscious and unconscious bias as well as our privileges. Understanding the ways in which we have advantages compared to others will help us start to uncover the ways we can use our privilege to impact change for those who do not have those same privileges.

I would also encourage listening sessions as a way to build racial empathy, awareness, and understanding. Listening sessions can be thought of as open forums where employees are invited to share their feelings, opinions and emotions around a specific issue or topic. It's important for listening sessions to be facilitated by someone with skill and expertise. Many organizations I've worked with have implemented listening sessions into their DEI strategy, however, I will point out that it's important for listening sessions to be an ongoing part of company practice. With the racial unrest that reached a tipping point during the summer of 2020, many companies decided to conduct listening sessions following the tragic stories of Ahmaud Arbery, George Floyd, Breonna Taylor and Jacob Blake. Again, listening sessions should not just occur after an incident involving trauma or death but should be woven into the fabric of the organization.

Listening sessions are beneficial because they encourage active listening and dialogue. Active listening is a vital aspect of productive racial dialogue. Sharpening listening skills will create individuals who are more, what I would call racially astute, which is a term I've coined. Being racially astute means you have a deep awareness and understanding of how different historical events have impacted and shaped the experiences of different racial groups .

A lot of organizations and institutions have implemented employee book clubs as a way to open up discussions about race. I think book clubs are a good way to open racial dialogue but there are other ways to open up these types of conversations. Reading can be an effective and impactful way to boost empathy but not everyone enjoys reading. Book clubs are great but are limited to those who actually want to read and participate. In my first book, *Dirty Diversity*, I shared that book clubs are a way to boost understanding, which I still stand by. I want to offer some additional options for your anti-racism efforts. Discussions around movies, television shows, and podcasts, are a creative way to open up racial dialogue. As previously mentioned, anti-racism education should include the Consume, Digest & Dialogue (CDD) activity. Watching a documentary like *13th*, which can currently be found on Netflix, and having a discussion on different parts of the documentary is a great way to boost awareness and understanding. Leadership should customize anti-racism education to fit the specific needs of the organization and also be open to outside-of-the-box strategies.

CHAPTER 8

HOW TO SUPPORT
YOUR BLACK EMPLOYEES

Following the Racial Revolution of 2020, organizations have realized that there must be a specific focus placed on Black employees and what is being done to support them. Many companies were accused of *performative allyship*, or hopping on the anti-racism bandwagon because it was trendy. Now more than ever, employees are holding their employer's proverbial feet to the fire and making them more accountable for their diversity pledges and promises. Hiring managers will now have to navigate questions like "what is your company's stance on the Black Lives Matter movement?" and "what are you currently doing to support Black employees?" These are very important questions and the purpose of this chapter is to provide actionable ways to support Black employees in your workplace. I speak as one Black, millennial woman and do not speak for all Black people as Black people are not a monolith. One of the most frequent questions I've gotten since the Racial Revolution began is "how can we support our Black employees?" With the continued Black death and trauma that is playing 24/7 on the news cycle while compounded by the global pandemic, organizational leaders must gain a better understanding of this to truly foster equity and inclusion.

To answer this question of how to support Black employees, there must be an understanding of how Black people in America have been harmed, disadvantaged and marginalized for hundreds of years. The perception is that when Abraham Lincoln signed the Emancipation Proclamation, enslaved people were finally free, but this wasn't the case. Although the Emancipation Proclamation was signed in 1863 and granted the freedom of enslaved persons in the U.S., in some parts of the country slaves were still not free. Every system built in the U.S. was meant to keep Black people out. The electoral college, a system designed to select the U.S. president, is another structure that is steeped in racism. A large part of the reason why there was pushback with adopting the popular vote system for choosing the president is because the original framers of the constitution felt that slaveholding southern states would be at a disadvantage because of the amount of their population that was enslaved and therefore could not vote. The solution was to adopt the three-fifths compromise, which specified that each enslaved Black person would count as three-fifths of a white person. The irony is that enslaved people were not able to vote yet they were being used as leverage and incentivized slaveholding states$_1$. Understanding how to support your Black employees requires you to understand how these systems of oppression have worked to disenfranchise Black people since the country's inception.

From the moment a Black person applies for a job, there are factors that work against them to keep them out. Name bias is a prevalent issue where recruiters and hiring managers discriminate against candidates that have more Black-sounding names. There have been several studies that verify that this is still a problem in the modern workplace. Aside from unconscious racial bias, where a person may be deemed unsuitable for a role because of the color of their skin, barriers to entry must be mitigated. Once in the workplace, Black people, and Black women in particular, are more likely to be tone policed when sharing feelings or experiences of differential treatment. In many industries, Black people are less likely to be promoted for senior leadership roles within the company. This often leads to an overrepresentation of Black people in junior roles in the company while there is a lack of representation as you move up in the organization. Rapper Jay-Z described it like a domino. A domino is a great metaphor for senior leadership in corporate America-mostly white with a few Black people sprinkled throughout. A result of the Racial Revolution of 2020 is that more companies are realizing that there must be a concerted effort to understand and support Black employees. You can no longer lump all employees of color together and assume that BIPOC are a monolith. There are unique challenges that Black people face that must be considered. Here are some ways to support your Black employees to ensure you are creating an environment where they feel valued, respected and included.

Mentorship and Sponsorship programs: A 2019 study conducted by Coqual found that nearly one in five Black employees surveyed felt like it would be challenging for someone of their race/ethnicity to achieve a senior leadership role within their company. Black employees are frustrated with the lack of advancement opportunities[2]. Two ways to remedy this is creating mentorship and/or sponsorship programs in the workplace. Mentorship programs can come in many shapes and forms but essentially junior employees are paired with more senior-level employees who serve as mentors and provide guidance. A sponsorship program takes things a step further. Sponsors serve as an active advocate for the individual they are paired with. Sponsorship takes on a more participatory role in an individual's success, whereas mentorship programs are more hands-off and often centers around providing mentees with guidance and advice that can help them navigate their careers. Both mentorship and sponsorship programs can help propel the career of Black employees by providing them with the guidance and tools needed to advance in their career. Every organization should think about how these programs can be implemented.

Employee Resource Groups: To create an inclusive and equitable environment for all employees, it is vital to create a safe space for people of all backgrounds. Many companies have found success with introducing employee resource groups (ERGs). These are groups of employees with shared characteristics (ethnicity, race, gender, religion, etc.) who come together and meet on a regular basis. A Black ERG can serve as that safe space for Black employees. It is imperative to ensure before establishing an ERG that there are clear objectives for what the purpose of the ERG is (fostering inclusion, allyship from non-Black people, etc.) and metrics are helpful to periodically assess whether the group is accomplishing its stated objectives. Defining the Objectives and Key Results (OKRs) can be helpful. The objective would be what the purpose or goals of the group are and the key results would be the metric that is being used to measure each of the objectives or goals. Developing a few OKRs at the inception of the ERG will allow the group to be successful.

Listen to Black employees: One of the best ways to support Black employees may be the most simplistic: listen to your Black employees. Take a pulse of how they are feeling. This can be done in a number of different ways. Surveys are helpful. On the surveys, employees can (if they feel comfortable) identify their race so that survey analysis can assess whether there are racial differences in results. Surveys can assess the culture of inclusion that the organization is fostering and allow respondents to leave feedback.

In addition, leadership can analyze exit interview data to see whether there are trends in what employees who leave the organization are saying about the climate within the company. Exit interview data is an underutilized resource that companies should take advantage of. In addition to exit interview data, if your company has a Black ERG, invite them to share their feedback with company executives

Address racial microaggressions: Every organization should have different ways to navigate and deal with racial microaggressions. It is imperative to have frequent and open forums and sessions where employees and organizational leaders can have conversations about microaggressions. Someone with expertise should be leading and facilitating these conversations. They should take place often and continuously (I would recommend once a month sessions).

More education is needed around issues that negatively impact the Black community, like hair discrimination. Currently, there are no federal protections for discrimination of Black hair. In most U.S. states, it is perfectly legal for an organization to prohibit employees from rocking hairstyles that are deemed "too Afrocentric." There have been countless cases where Black employees are told that they must change their hairstyles or face negative consequences and in the majority of these cases the courts have sided with the companies and not the Black employee. Addressing the different ways that microaggressions can manifest will be instrumental in increasing awareness and understanding from non-Black employees.

Understand misogynoir. Malcolm X is quoted to have said that the most disrespected person in America is the Black woman[3]. Misogynoir is a term coined by Dr. Moya Bailey to describe the distinct form of oppression that Black women face[4]. Black women have to navigate the combined effects of racism and sexism. Anti-black racism is an issue all Black people experience but for Black women experiences with oppression are intensified with sexism. Efforts to close the gender divide must take into consideration misogynoir and Black women's experiences navigating the 'angry Black woman' stereotype as well as how issues like tone policing create additional challenges. Black women have to navigate what is called the concrete ceiling, or the invisible barriers that impact advancement. Going back to the previous point about the importance of listening to Black employees, it is important to listen to the specific issues raised by Black women in your workplace. Recognize ways that misogynoir may manifest and impact Black women. To paraphrase the words of the members of the Combahee River Collective, when Black women are free, all other groups of people will be free₅.

In recent years, one trend I've seen that deserves an honorable mention is what I'd like to call the Paul Mooney syndrome. Paul Mooney is a comedian who speaks often about Black culture and race and is famously quoted as saying "everybody wanna be Black, but don't nobody wanna be

Black." My interpretation of this statement is that people want parts of Blackness without actually having to experience the negative aspects of Blackness, such as racism. Rachel Dolezal may be a good example of the Paul Mooney syndrome. Dolezal is a white woman who engaged in what you could 'blackfishing' where she manipulated her appearance to pass as a Black person. There have been other instances of non-black people claiming to be biracial or fully Black because of the perceived benefits associated. While there is no marker for what it means to be Black or who can call themselves Black, it is important to understand how problematic it is when Blackness is used as a way to gain clout, validity, authority or authenticity. Falsely claiming Black/African ancestry as a badge of honor to gain access or acceptance in any way is troublesome. Blackness is not something you can claim when it's convenient for you. This is a phenomenon I call Black coating, where people try on Blackness to see how it fits and then take it off when it no longer suits them. Understanding how Blackness is often manipulated and capitalized upon will help you better understand Black people's experiences.

Black coating is the claim of Blackness when it's convenient for an individual. Over the years, I've seen several public figures from outside of the Black community, who have been called out for anti-black behavior. When called out, these public figures cling to their partial African ancestry, which they never claimed until it was convenient for them. A new phenomenon within the last few years that has gained popularity is blackfishing. Blackfishing is the act of altering one's appearance to resemble that of a Black person to gain popularity, status, sponsorship deals or other perceived benefits. Blackfishing is a form of Black coating that I see frequently on social media. Several white influencers have been called out for blackfishing, which has helped them gain visibility online. Blackfishing and Black coating are aimed at taking the parts of Blackness that are desirable and adopting these characteristics for personal gain. Blackfishing and Black coating are another way that those with privilege capitalize on their access and opportunity to the detriment of Black people. Oftentimes, the perpetrators are taking opportunities from actual Black people. Some have argued that Blackfishing and Black coating are forms of Blackface. Blackface was a minstrel show that gained popularity during the 18th century. White people would darken their skin and draw on large cartoonish lips to mimic that of a Black person in order to play Black characters and display exaggerated and negative stereotypes about Black people[6].

It seems like the world is embracing Black culture and identity and there is a collective "wokeness" that is shifting people's perspectives but it's important to mention that some efforts are more performative and virtue signalling. Many people want to appear as if they are racially conscious for the perceived benefits that are associated with it. You want to avoid doing things for cosmetic purposes, which many companies have been called out for in the wake of the Racial Revolution of 2020. Organizations truly committed to creating an environment where Black employees are supported and valued must make sure that every promise is followed by direct action. The black squares that were posted on social media following the killing of George Floyd were one step, but what did your company follow that action with?

For years, the needs, desires, and challenges that Black employees faced were not highlighted or were jumbled in with all other people of color. The aforementioned study by Coqual also found that many Black professionals are frustrated with the 'person of color' designation given to all non-white racial groups. I agree that the labeling of white versus non-white can prevent people from fully understanding the unique systemic challenges that different racial groups in the U.S. have endured. In the past, Black issues have often been overlooked or swept under the rug, with DEI efforts focused on all people of color or women. The Racial Revolution of 2020 brought to the forefront the need for companies to understand Black employees and how there is a disconnect as far as needs, wants, and desires and what allyship, advocacy and support look like to this group. To understand Black employees better, first recognize that people of color are not a monolith. The challenges that Black people in America have endured are unlike any other racial group in America. Take every opportunity you are given to learn about the Black community and what we have experienced in the U.S. There must be a more nuanced approach when seeking to understand Black people.

CHAPTER 9

---◁◆▷---

BREAKING THE HABIT
OF SYSTEMIC RACISM

To create an anti-racist workplace, we must break our habits of racism. We've explored strategies to unpack our individual racism and recognize our blindspots but as an organization, systemic changes will not occur until we fix the structures from which racism is able to thrive. What policies, practices, and procedures can be implemented into your workplace to create and foster an anti-racist workplace?

- **Setting goals**: If your company is truly committed to creating an anti-racist organization, goal-setting is imperative. What does racial equity look like in your company? Clearly define what your goals are and utilize S.M.A.R.T. goal-setting strategies to develop clear DEI objectives. The S.M.A.R.T. acronym stands for specific, measurable, attainable, relevant, and time bound. Racial equity goals should be clearly defined and assessed on a consistent basis. The act of simply setting goals and writing them down increases the likelihood of goal attainment. In addition to setting goals, to get leadership more invested in fostering racial equity, these specific goals should be tied to executive pay or bonuses. Breaking the habit of racism in your organization requires a clear understanding of the specific race-related issues and what aspects of your workplace are creating barriers to racial equity and inclusion. Once these barriers are clearly defined, create specific objectives for how to overcome these obstacles.

- **Greater objectivity**: Assess every system and structure within the organization. What are the daily practices and procedures? Evaluate what the processes are for each of these procedures and policies and then analyze whether these processes are objective. Does your company, for example, utilize a rubric when evaluating job candidates or job performance? A rubric is a scorecard that hiring managers can use to make less biased decisions when hiring candidates.

During a job interview, a rubric is used to evaluate a job candidate and assess whether they possess the knowledge, skills and abilities needed for a particular role. Having specific and measurable criteria for evaluating individuals can be an effective strategy to foster racial equity. In addition, structured interviews can mitigate the unconscious bias that tends to creep into the hiring and selection process. Assess each company procedure and investigate whether these processes and procedures are objective, fair and equitable.

- **Create a diverse pipeline**: Organizations must take an active role in developing a racially diverse pipeline. Many companies complain about their inability to find diverse talent yet many organizations are doing little to ensure that diverse candidates are being attracted to the organization. If there is an apparent lack of diverse candidates in your pool, what systems can be created to ensure that underrepresented groups are attracted to the organization? Apprenticeship and internship programs are two ways to create direct access to potential candidates. Apprenticeship programs often involve equipping interested candidates with the hands-on skills necessary to be skilled in a particular industry. Internship programs are also a great way to attract diverse talent but the key to remember is that internships should be paid. Candidates from underrepresented racial backgrounds don't often have the luxury of working an unpaid internship so unpaid internships may unintentionally discourage applicants of color from applying. Be proactive about building a diverse talent pool so that you are able to impact diverse representation at the company. Building an anti-racist workplace involves not only engaging in activities that foster racial equity and inclusion but also dismantling practices that may be keeping people out of the company.

- **Hold racists accountable**: It's important to draw a clear line in the sand to indicate to employees that your organization does not tolerate racism in any way, shape or form. Employees that engage in hate speech or racist behaviors must be disciplined. There is no one-size-fits-all playbook for when to fire a racist versus when to take disciplinary action against someone who shows racist tendencies. When something is said or done that is considered racially offensive, it is imperative that it's addressed in one way or another. The only way to create an anti-racist organization is to hold people who perpetuate racism accountable. No matter how many impactful policies, practices and procedures are implemented into the organization, if racists are able to advance and thrive within the company, you will never be able to create an anti-racist workplace.

- **Recognize some of the common racial/ethnic microaggressions**: It is important to understand some common racial microaggressions that can sabotage a conversation and make a person feel othered. This is by no means an exhaustive list but simply a starting point for you to gain a deeper understanding of what some current racial/ethnicity microaggressions are.

    o *Telling a BIPOC that they are articulate or that they "speak good English"*: This is offensive because it signals to the BIPOC that they are a deviation from the norm. The implication in this statement is that people from their race/ethnicity are generally *not* articulate and that this person is an aberration. Telling a person that they "speak good English" without having a full understanding of upbringing is microaggressive and again makes a person feel slighted. The underlying implication is that the person is "other" and that their native language cannot possibly be English.

o *Describing yourself as 'colorblind':* We explored this topic earlier in the book but it's important to reiterate this: while your intentions may be good and you were raised 'not to see color' and to see people for the content of their character, the reality of it is that if we have eyes that can see, we all see color. If you do not see race, how will you be able to spot racism? Rather than adopting this belief of being colorblind (a false belief and misnomer) it is important to understand that the goal is to refrain from making decisions based on a person's skin color.

o *Asking to shorten a person's name because you cannot pronounce it:* Many people have changed, modified or shortened their name (including myself) for the purposes of assimilation and being able to gain acceptance by the white majority. Countless research studies have indicated that name discrimination is still a prevalent issue in the U.S. and beyond and those with "more ethnic" sounding names often experience bias during the hiring process. Understand the long history of name discrimination and how it impacts communities of color. Rather than asking someone to call them by a nickname, allyship involves taking the time and effort to actually learn a person's name. Make an effort to write it down if you think you will forget the pronunciation. LinkedIn created a cool new feature where you can record the pronunciation of your name for your profile. I love this feature because often-times my first and last names are mispronounced. Take the time to learn a person's name, no matter how complicated you may think it is, and refrain from using nicknames (unless explicitly told by the individual to do so)

o *Asking to touch a Black person's hair:* Everyone should refrain from doing this. With the vast number of hairstyles I've rocked, this is a question I get more often than I'd like. Asking to touch a Black person's hair makes us feel put on display. Before asking a Black person to touch their hair, ask yourself if that's a question you'd be asking if the person was of another race. The likely answer is no. Understanding the dark history of Black people being put on display should provide a clear indication for why this is an offensive question to ask a Black person. Sara Baartman was a South African woman who, in the 1800s was put on display in Europe as a tourist attraction. Baartman was ogled and objectified because of the size of her buttocks[1]. Also, in the early 1900s, an African man was put on display in New York, due to his boyish appearance$_2$. When you ask a Black person if you can touch our hair, it reinforces the stereotype of Black people being 'other.' It makes us feel like pets. If you are fascinated by a person's hair, explain this to them, and you can inquire about the hairstyle or do your own online searching to learn more about it.

o *Asking a person "what are you?"* This is a question often posed to a multiracial or racially ambiguous person and can make them feel uncomfortable. During a training session, someone shared with me that he gets asked this question a lot and it makes him feel like an object. If you're curious about a person's ethnicity, there are other ways to go about asking about it in a more polite way. You can inquire about what a person's heritage is, or ask a person what their background is.

o *Using the term spirit animal:* It recently came to my attention that the term spirit animal is actually highly problematic.

People often use the term to describe someone that they connect with or that they admire or see part of themselves in. Someone might say something like "Beyonce is my spirit animal." The term is derived from the culture of Indigenous peoples in the U.S. (also known as Native Americans) and is used to describe a spirit that serves as a guide to someone going through a difficulty$_3$. Animals play an important role in the culture and those outside the culture have taken a meaningful term and turned it into something that degrades its original meaning.. Instead of using the term spirit animal, you can say someone matches your vibe or that they are on the same frequency or wavelength as you. While we're on the topic, another problematic phrase you may have grown up hearing is the word *powwow*. The term is meant to mean a gathering of people but in Indigenous American culture, powwows are more intricate gatherings and celebrations. The common usage of the term, demeans the amount of planning that goes into these celebrations and again degrades and downplays the original meaning. Along these same lines, a phrase that must be abolished is the phrase "too many chiefs, not enough Indians."

- Outdated Race/Ethnicity Categories:
  - **Oriental**: This was a term that was often used to describe a person from East Asia, particularly countries like China, Japan, Korea, and surrounding nations. According to a *Los Angeles Times* opinion article by Jayne Tsuchiyama, the word is problematic because it "makes Asians sound exotic[4]." As a general rule of thumb, if you know the specific country that a person is from, it's always best to refer to people based on this. Asian is a catch-all term used to describe anyone from the continent of Asia. Instead of using the term Asian, which is more general and can tend to be vague, region-based descriptors can be better. The term South Asian is used to refer to

people from countries like India, Pakistan, Bangladesh, Sri Lanka, Nepal and other surrounding countries. In the past, I've used the term Oriental without realizing its problematic nature, but once you know better it is your responsibility to do better and to educate others.

o **Native American:** Although this term is still heavily used, the preferred term is Indigenous Peoples. It's important to state the country of origin for the Indigenous people since the term simply means the original peoples of a particular country or area.

o **African American**: Decades ago, the term African American was preferred, but currently it's a somewhat outdated term to describe Black people within the United States. The reason why the term is outdated is that it's not fully accurate or descriptive. A close friend of mine from St. Lucia indicated that she's not a fan of the term because she considers herself a Caribbean immigrant therefore the term African American, she feels, does not fully represent her. Personally, I prefer the term Black because there's less confusion on what that means and it's a universal term to describe a person of African origins and ancestry. African American is also not an accurate description of someone of African descent who grew up in a different country, like a British Ghanaian, for example.

o **Aboriginal/Aborigine:** This is a term used to describe the Indigenous peoples of Australia. The term is considered less accurate and is being phased out because the term Aborigine has a history of being used as a racial slur and both of these terms disregard the history of the Indigenous people before they were colonized. Aboriginal was not a term used to describe the Indigenous peoples of Australia until European invasion. Instead, use terms like the Indigenous Australian people or the original people of Australia.

o **Spanish:** This word is being phased out and replaced with Hispanic, a term used to describe individuals from Spanish-speaking countries and Latinx, a gender neutral term used to describe people from Latin America. Again, if you know the specific country where a person is from, it's always best to use the country to describe a person's ethnicity. Saying "she is from Panama" instead of saying "she is Hispanic" is better. Also note that Hispanic/Latinx is not a race but rather an ethnicity. A person can be both Latinx and Black (Afro-Latinx).

While on the topic of racial and ethnic categories, it's important to have a conversation about the difference between race and ethnicity because they are often conflated terms but mean two different things. Race is a social construct that is used to describe a person's skin color, phenotype, hair texture and other physical characteristics. The U.S. Census Bureau designates five different racial categories: White, Black or African American, American Indian or Alaska Native, Asian, Native Hawaiian or Other Pacific₅. A person can also be biracial (mixed with two different races) or multiracial (mixed with multiple races). Ethnicity, on the other hand, refers to the shared language, traditions, values, religion, and cultural norms shared by a group of people. A person's country of national origin is sometimes used as a way to describe their ethnicity. My parents immigrated to the U.S. from the West African country of Cameroon. My ethnicity is Cameroonian. My race is Black. Understanding that race and ethnicity are different is critical. Recognizing the difference between race and ethnicity will lead to a deeper awareness of a person's unique experiences.

A person can be part of a marginalized ethnic group but can still reap and enjoy the benefits of white privilege. Having a shared ethnicity doesn't mean your experiences are the same. In the Latinx community, white-presenting Latinx people have different experiences and advantages compared to Afro-Latinx people. An Afro-Latinx person identifies with a country in Latin America based on shared culture and values but may also experience discrimination based on their skin color. I have often heard the narrative that a person who identifies as Hispanic or Latinx cannot be racist because they are a person of color but it's important to first understand that being of a particular ethnicity doesn't excuse you from racism because again ethnicity and race are two different things.

It's important to also understand that Black is not just associated with the U.S. The Melanesian people, for example, are an ethnic group of Indigenous peoples that were populated in different Pacific Islands including New Guinea, Fiji, and the Solomon Islands$_6$. Melanesia translates in Greek to mean the Black islands. Melanesian people are Black by race but Melanesian by ethnicity. The Siddi people are an ethnic group that is mostly found in Pakistan and India. The Siddis descended from the Bantu peoples in Africa$_7$. Siddis are also Black by race. No matter what ethnicity you are, you can perpetuate anti-black racism.

- It's also important to be mindful of terms that can be considered racialized or having racial undertones. In politics, this is called a dog whistle, which can be thought of as a term that conjures up an image of a particular group without having to specify or state the group explicitly. Oftentimes, politicians use dog whistles that are racialized. Some specific examples of racialized words that you should be aware of include:

- Terrorist: Many people associate this word with a person who is Arab, Middle Eastern, North African and Muslim. This word rose in popularity in 2001 following the attacks that occurred on September 11th. Nearly 20 years later, people still associate this word with people from a particular region of the world.

- Nappy: This term is almost exclusively used to describe Black hair. In my first book *Dirty Diversity*, I shared a story of a close friend of mine who used the term to describe a popular Black singer's hair. I pushed back against the usage of the word because it's pejorative and more derogatory in nature. What I find highly problematic is the usage of this word amongst communities of color and particularly Black communities. We must remove this word from our vernacular.

- Ghetto: This term originally meant neighborhoods in different parts of Europe where Jewish people were forced to live. Ghettos tended to be places of high poverty and crowded quarters with deplorable living conditions. In the 21st century, the term has morphed and changed to mean a lower-income area of a big city, typically populated by Black and Hispanic communities. The term is more derogatory in nature and is usually considered to be an insult. The word has taken on new meaning and can either be used to describe a poverty-stricken area of a city or as an adjective to describe a person who is low-class or less educated.

o Thug: This originated as a Hindi word and the original meaning was someone who was a thief or cheater[8]. The word has morphed in present day to be a coded way of describing a Black person or Hispanic/Latinx person involved in perceived criminal activity and is definitely more derogatory in nature.

o Illegal immigrant: Referring to an undocumented immigrant as 'illegal' increases the anti-immigrant sentiment that often manifests into bias against

Mexicans and those from neighboring countries.

o Gypsy: This commonly used word is known to mean a person who is free-spirited and lives what one would call a vagabond lifestyle, moving from place to place without a solid homebase. The word originated from Europeans who used the word to describe the Romani people, an ethnic group that came to Europe from India. The Europeans thought that the Romani people were Egyptian because of their features. To-day the term is considered to be pejorative and offensive[9]. Also important to be mindful of is the word 'gypped' which is a derivative of the word gypsy and means to swindle or cheat someone[10].

The Pyramid of Racism in the Workplace

Created by Janice Z. Gassam Asare, Ph.D.

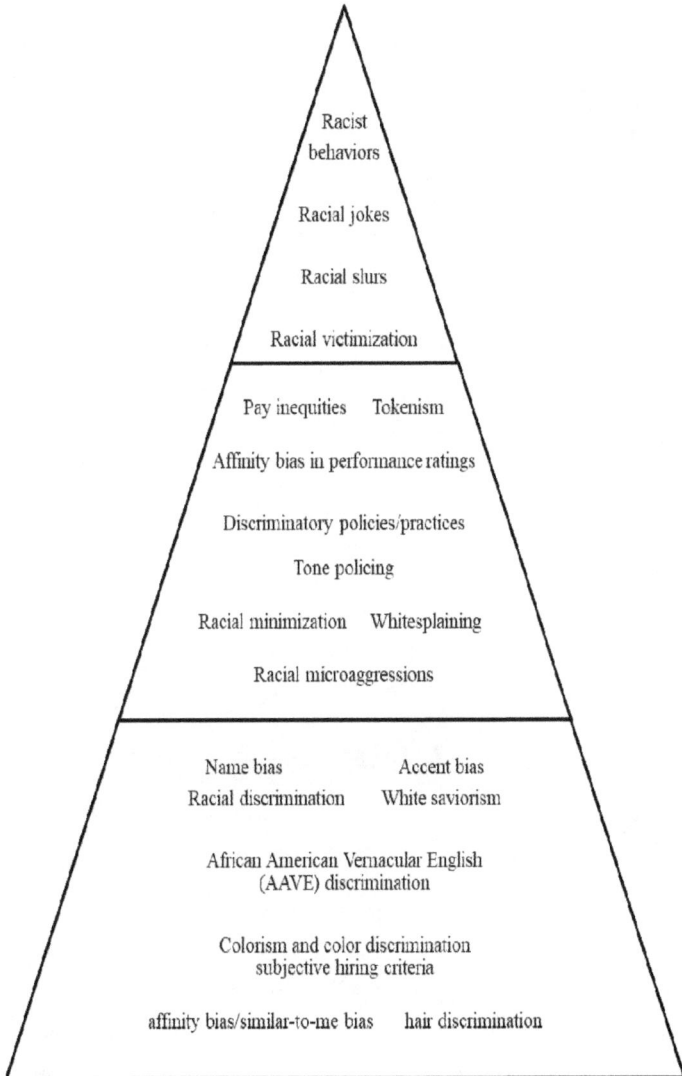

Racist
behaviors

Racial jokes

Racial slurs

Racial victimization

Pay inequities   Tokenism

Affinity bias in performance ratings

Discriminatory policies/practices

Tone policing

Racial minimization   Whitesplaining

Racial microaggressions

Name bias   Accent bias
Racial discrimination   White saviorism

African American Vernacular English
(AAVE) discrimination

Colorism and color discrimination
subjective hiring criteria

affinity bias/similar-to-me bias   hair discrimination

Issues that are not addressed at the lower level of the pyramid, build up and accrue to cause damage and greater issues. As you move further up on the pyramid, you see what these behaviors can manifest into.

CHAPTER 10

———⋘◆⋙———

FREQUENTLY ASKED QUESTIONS IN THE WORKPLACE

In my racial equity workshops, I include an activity called the Ask Me Anything (AMA) session. I invite questions about diversity, equity and inclusion but more specifically questions that people may have about race, racism, and the Black community. I always preface it by saying that I am one Black woman and don't speak for or represent the entire Black community but I offer these responses as a way to glean insights to burning questions people have always wondered about. This chapter comprises some of the frequently asked questions I've received from AMA sessions. This section will contain both the questions asked as well as my written responses to the questions posed.

Question 1: *Should people be hired based on skin color?*

Response: I would never advocate for hiring a person based on their skin color. There is a common misconception that Affirmative Action programs provide unqualified BIPOC applicants with jobs. The reality is that the purpose of these programs is to show preference to an **equally qualified** candidate from a historically disadvantaged background. The operative words are *equally qualified*. It's never a good practice to hire someone because you need to increase your diverse representation. That will leave employees resentful against the company but also, employees may not be welcoming to a new employee based on the perception that the employee is not qualified. Similarly, a BIPOC who was hired simply because of their race will also be left feeling tokenized and may start questioning their value and worth in the organization. Choose candidates based on who is the best person for the job while also implementing practices that will ensure there is diverse representation in your talent pool.

Question 2: *Will the learning ever stop? I'm nervous that because of the climate that we're in, I have to walk on eggshells and I don't want to offend anyone.*

Response: It's important to understand and to re-member that we will always make mistakes. The learning never stops and we must be continuously engaged in the learning process. It's not realistic to think once we've started on this journey that we will never offend anyone but with greater awareness comes adaptability. We must open ourselves up to possible criticism because on the other side of that is growth, learning and greater understanding.

Question 3: *How do you actually get leadership on board with creating more racial equity in the workplace?*

Response: It sounds odd to say that some people don't see the humanity in others and that you must show them why these issues matter. Ultimately, a workplace that does not foster a safe environment for all employees or make them feel a sense of be-longing and value will not thrive. I think part of the reason why people "don't care" about these issues is because of the false belief that it does not actually affect them. Getting leadership to understand how issues of racism affect everyone is vital. From a fi-nancial standpoint, a toxic work culture is not sus-tainable in the long term. Now, more than ever, employees feel empowered and comfortable outing employers for racist behaviors and empty promises. That should be incentive enough to get leadership to get with the program. Some companies have found success linking executive pay with diversity goals, so that may be something to think about within your organization. Also, people are naturally more invested when they are instrumental in developing a program or a set of initiatives. Racial equity is everyone's responsibility but especially those in leadership positions. Leadership should be helping the Diversity Manager or Chief Diversity Officer to develop equity programs and initiatives.

Question 4: *I would love to learn more about cultural appropriation. How can you distinguish appreciation from appropriation?*

Response: Some people will disagree with me and say if you are not of a culture you should not mimic the culture, even if it's done from a place of admiration. In my personal opinion, I think if you decide to wear a style that is from another culture, be sure to give proper credit. It is appropriation when things are stolen from the cultures from whence they were created, without giving proper credit to said culture. This is what I would call a whitewashing of history. Country music, for example, is said to have been derived from 17th century slave ships[1]. Enslaved people had instruments that were brought from their home countries and were used to entertain the slave masters. Country music is a great example of a musical genre that has its origins and roots in African culture, yet many people do not know this and African/Black culture is rarely ever cited as being the origin of the genre. It could be argued that this is a form of cultural appropriation because of the lack of credit that is given. Taking from another culture and trying to pass it off as your creation or wrongly citing the origin of the inspiration is when you venture into appropriation territory.

While on the topic of appropriation, a somewhat similar and relevant topic to also explore is digital blackface. Blackface, as we've discussed, were minstrel shows that were popularized in the 1800s. White people would get shoe polish and other substances to darken their skin and they would paint cartoonish lips on themselves to play roles as Black people, adopting and acting out exaggerated and negative stereotypes. Digital blackface can be thought of as a version of blackface through the use of GIFs. People have been using GIFs and more specifically, reaction GIFs, throughout the last few years as a way to convey different emotions. Some have argued that digital blackface is problematic because of the perpetuation and glorification of Black stereotypes. Some of the most popular reaction GIFs are of Black people displaying a wide range of exaggerated emotions from annoyance and anger to excitement and surprise. These GIFs play into many stereotypes about Black people including being ghetto, angry, and sassy and may reinforce the unconscious biases and subtle prejudice we have about Black people$_2$. Being mindful of digital blackface and how it can strengthen and reinforce our negative stereotypes is vital to understand and explore. There is no specific guideline for when digital blackface should and shouldn't be used but I would suggest exercising caution as a non-black person using digital blackface.

Question 5: *I am white and haven't had a privileged life. Can you explain the term white privilege?*

Response: In my experiences, there has been some difficulty in understanding the term *white privi-*

lege. White privilege is the invisible access and opportunities that a person in society receives because of their white skin. Privilege has nothing to do with wealth or upbringing. You may have grown up in a lower-income neighborhood and still have white privilege, which has made your experiences different from your non-white counterparts. I believe that there is difficulty understanding white privilege because the word privilege sparks guilt in some people. Having white privilege doesn't make you a bad person. Understanding that you have this privilege and then not doing anything about it is what's problematic. An alternative term to white privilege that I would encourage and may conceptualize this concept more clearly is white advantage. Some specific examples of white advantage that I've experienced: Years ago, I worked in an organization where we each had our own offices. My colleagues were mostly PhDs like myself and therefore they all had "Dr" in front of their name on their office door. When my colleagues and I received our new offices, I noticed that my door was the only door that did not have the "Dr" in front of it, even though I was a PhD like my white, male counterparts. It took awhile for my name to be changed.

The only things that separated me from my coworkers were gender and skin color. I was the only Black person in the department. Perhaps it was an oversight by the administrative assistant but it felt more like a racial microaggression that my white male colleagues did not have to experience.

A more egregious incident also happened several years ago, when I was applying to a job I was highly qualified for. A less qualified white candidate got the job over me. I had everything that they were looking for including the experience, education and a personal connection at the organization, however, I was passed over for the job. The organization instead hired a white woman who was not qualified for the job. I was told by my personal connection that although she had less education and no relevant experience, they felt like she "fit" the organization better than I did. The only explanation I can think of as to why she got the job over me was skin color. White advantage can work in a number of different ways from getting job opportunities to being given the benefit of the doubt when being pulled over. Lacking salary or status doesn't mean one lacks invisible advantages that create different experiences than those without these advantages.

Question 6: *Will I always feel white guilt?*

Response: White guilt is often sparked by a recognition and understanding of what was described earlier as white advantage. For many, white guilt was sparked during the Racial Revolution of 2020. Again, there is nothing wrong with having advantage, but what is important to understand is that once you have the realization that you have access, opportunities and advantages that others do not have, it is your responsibility and duty to impact change. If you are feeling guilty, ask yourself how you can channel that guilt into change. Guilt is okay, if it is followed by action. Decenter your feelings from the conversation and focus on how to use your feelings of guilt to invoke change.

Question 7: *What will it take to produce actual change following the assassination of George Floyd?*

Response: This is an important question we must continually ask ourselves. I think this moment is much different than other time periods when there was social unrest. Following the murder of Trayvon Martin in 2012 and after the killing of Mike Brown in 2014, there were mass protests, national conversations but then the conversations simmered. Because the racial pandemic has been happening in the backdrop of the global pandemic of Covid-19, everything erupted in an unimaginable way. People are hungry for change and really want this world to heal and get better. Employees are not settling with empty promises followed by little action. Continued conversations about racial equity and inclusion are imperative to ensure that this issue stays at the forefront and we continue to develop strategies for more long term change. We cannot let things fizzle out like they have in the past. We must continue to hold our leadership accountable and keep this issue in the public conversation for systemic changes to be made.

THE PINK ELEPHANT QUICK REFERENCE GUIDE

Historical Racism (Chapter 2)

- Indian Removal Act of 1830
- Special Order No. 15
- Chinese Exclusion Act
- Separate but Equal
- The Immigration Act of 1924

Understanding Race and Racism

- Consume, Digest & Dialogue activity (Chapter 2)
- Racially astute (Chapter 7)

When Unpacking and Understanding Advantages and Privilege

- White privilege (Chapter 4)
- White adjacency (Chapter 4)
- Advantage Awareness Activity (Chapter 7)

Strategies for Effective Racial Dialogue (Chapter 5)

- Assess, Discuss, Repeat (A.D.R.)
- Accept, Own, Correct (A.O.C.)

Racial Dialogue Derailers (Chapter 6)

- White centering
- Whataboutism
- White denial
- White gaze
- Tone policing
- Racial gaslighting
- White defensiveness
- Adopting a fixed mindset
- Whitesplaining
- White saviorism
- The weaponization of whiteness
- Racial minimization

Other Important Terms to Understand (Chapter 8)

- Performative allyship
- Misogynoir
- Paul Mooney Syndrome
- Black coating

EPILOGUE:

I understand that there was a lot to unpack in this book. My hope is that you use this as a guidebook that you can continuously refer to. Use this as a resource to help you when having conversations with coworkers. If you found this book insightful, please gift it to others. My goal is to plant seeds into the world that will grow into change. Remember that you must continuously be strengthening your anti-racism muscles. Use this book as a tool to open conversations and bridge gaps in your workplace. The more we are able to have these conversations, the closer your organization will be to creating racial equity and inclusion. Creating an anti-racist workplace starts with education and dialogue, followed by action and systemic change. It is not enough to simply read this book but put these words into practice. I'm happy you've chosen to learn from me and I encourage you to share what you've learned with others. As a token of my appreciation, I have created a complimentary checklist of *5 Strategies to*

Create a Racially Equitable Workplace, which can be found on my website www.drjanicegassam.com/antiracism.

References

Chapter 2:

1. https://www.history.com/topics/native-american-history/trail-of-tears
2. https://www.georgiaencyclopedia.org/articl es/history-archaeology/shermans-field-order-no-15
3. https://www.history.com/topics/immigrati on/chinese-exclusion-act-1882
4. https://www.history.com/topics/black-history/plessy-v-ferguson
5. https://history.state.gov/milestones/1921-1936/immigration-act#:~:text=The%20Immigration%20Act%20of%201924%20limited%20the%20numb er%20of%20immigrants,of%20the%201890 %20national%20census.

Chapter 3:

1. https://swap.stanford.edu/2014121823001 6/http://mlk-

kpp01.stanford.edu/kingweb/popular_requ ests/frequentdocs/birmingham.pdf

2. https://www.collectiveliberation.org/wp-con-tent/uploads/2013/01/Smith_Heteropatria rchy_3_Pillars_of_White_Supremacy.pdf

3. https://www.mckinsey.com/~/media/Mc Kin-sey/Industries/Public%20and%20Social%2 0Sector/Our%20Insights/The%20economi c%20impact%20of%20closing%20the%20r acial%20wealth%20gap/The-economic-impact-of-closing-the-racial-wealth-gap-final.pdf

Chapter 4:

1. https://www.cnn.com/2019/10/22/us/lori -loughlin-felicity-huffman-fallout/index.html

2. https://www.npr.org/2011/01/28/133306 180/Mother-Jailed-For-School-Fraud-Flares-Controversy

3. https://www.nytimes.com/2019/04/30/us /minneapolis-police-noor-verdict.html

4. https://www.nytimes.com/2019/07/19/ny region/amadou-diallo-mother-eric-garner.html

5. https://www.nytimes.com/article/breonna-taylor-police.html

6. https://abcnews.go.com/US/key-moments-charleston-church-shooting-case-dylann-roof/story?id=46701033

7. https://abc7.com/dylann-roof-south-carolina-church-shooting-emanuel-african-methodist-episcopal/801013/

8. https://www.msn.com/en-us/news/us/what-we-know-about-george-floyds-death-and-alleged-counterfeit-money-in-minneapolis/ar-BB14ZqSZ

9. https://www.nytimes.com/2009/07/21/us/21gates.html

10. https://www.urbandictionary.com/define.php?term=White%20adjacent

Chapter 8

1. https://www.theatlantic.com/ideas/archive/2019/11/electoral-college-racist-origins/601918/

2. https://coqual.org/reports/being-black-in-corporateamerica-an-intersectional-exploration/

3. https://www.washingtonpost.com/local/where-areblack-men-in-the-fight-for-blackwomen/

4. 2018/11/13/63030e0c-e771-11e8-a939-9469f1166f9d_story.html

5. https://doi.org/10.1080/14680777.2018.1447395

6. https://www.newyorker.com/news/ourcolumnists/until-black-women-are-free-none-of-uswill-be-free

7. https://www.history.com/news/blackface-historyracism-origins

Chapter 9

1. https://www.bbc.com/news/magazine-35240987

2. https://www.cnn.com/2015/06/03/opinions/newkirk-bronx-zoo-man-cage/index.html

3. http://blog.nativepartnership.org/a-native-view-on-spirit-animals-and-animal-medicine/

4. https://www.latimes.com/opinion/op-ed/la-oe-tsuchiyama-oriental-insult-20160601-snap-story.html

5. https://www.census.gov/topics/population/race/about.html

6. https://www.britannica.com/place/Melanesia

7. http://www.bbc.com/travel/story/20160801-indias-forgotten-jungle-dwellers

8. https://www.newsweek.com/brief-history-word-thug-326595

9. https://now.org/blog/the-g-word-isnt-for-you-how-gypsy-erases-romani-women/

10. https://www.npr.org/sections/codeswitch/2013/12/30/242429836/why-being-gypped-hurts-the-roma-more-than-it-hurts-you

Chapter 10

1. https://www.washingtonpost.com/nation/2019/08/02/tracing-country-musics-roots-back-th-century-slave-ships/

2. https://www.teenvogue.com/story/digital-blackface-reaction-gifs